D1612417

Lighthouses

Lighthouses

DAVID ROSS

amber
BOOKS

First published in 2021

Copyright © 2021 Amber Books Ltd

All rights reserved. No part of this publication may be reproduced,
stored in a retrieval system, or transmitted in any form or by any
means, electronic, mechanical, photocopying, recording, or otherwise,
without prior written permission of the copyright holder.

Published by
Amber Books Ltd
United House
North Road
London
N7 9DP
United Kingdom
www.amberbooks.co.uk
Instagram: amberbooksltd
Facebook: amberbooks
Twitter: @amberbooks
Pinterest: amberbooksltd

Project Editor: Sarah Uttridge
Designers: Zoë Mellors
Picture Research: Terry Forshaw

ISBN: 978-1-83886-097-4

Printed in China

10503250

CORK
CITY
LIBRARIES

Contents

Introduction

A lighthouse can have two purposes: to signal 'Stay away', or 'Come this way'; warning against rocks and shallows, or guiding ships into a safe harbour. The first recorded lighthouse was at Alexandria in Egypt; one of the seven wonders of the ancient world, it was built around 280 BCE, lasted until 1323, and was 100m (330ft) high. For centuries, however, most coastal shipping had to rely on moonlight, or lay up for the night. The great era of lighthouse building began in the mid-18th century, stimulated by an increase in commercial shipping around the world's coastlines, and assisted by improvements in building techniques. These enabled storm-resistant towers to be erected in exposed and even wave-swept locations, with improved lights – first using oil, then gas and electricity – rather than open fires in braziers.

Originally, lighthouses required resident keepers, but in the course of the 20th century nearly all lighthouses were converted to automatic operation, with default lighting systems in the event of lamp failure. The occupation of lighthouse keeper has almost ceased to exist.

ABOVE:
Marshall Point Lighthouse, Maine, USA
OPPOSITE:
Newhaven Lighthouse, Newhaven, England

USA and Canada

Americans cherish their lighthouses. Although the advent of satellite navigation, radar and GPS has greatly reduced the number of active lighthouses in the past 30 years, local communities have adopted many that would have been demolished or left derelict. Renovated, they continue to serve as Private Aid to Navigation beacons, while also acting as iconic emblems for cities and counties.

The first American lighthouses were established in the colonial period, on the east coast, by both British and Dutch settlers. The first was at Boston Harbor, erected in 1716 and blown up in 1776 by British troops during the War of Independence. US lighthouse management passed to the Lighthouse Establishment (soon generally known as the Lighthouse Board) in 1789. In 1910, the Board was replaced by the Bureau of Lighthouses. This in turn was abolished in 1939 when the service was transferred to the US Coast Guard.

Canadian lighthouses, under the control of Fisheries and Oceans Canada, are also maintained and run by harbours and municipalities, frequently with the aid of voluntary groups.

OPPOSITE:
Eastern Point Lighthouse, Gloucester, Massachusetts, USA
Reached by a causeway formed of granite blocks, this 1890 tower is the third on the site. The white brick structure is 11m (36ft) high; automated in 1986, its beam is a white flash every five seconds.

Outer Light, Sodus Bay, New York State, USA
Spray breaks against the four-sided cast-iron tower in a Lake Ontario storm. The first tower here was a wooden one in 1872. Rebuilt in 1938 and reinforced by steel plating, 15m (49ft) high, it shows a fixed white light.

OPPOSITE:
Grand Haven Lighthouses, Michigan, USA
The first lighthouse on the south pier was built in 1839; the present steel-clad inner light, 11m (36ft) high, dates from 1905. The outer light building also held the fog signal apparatus.

LEFT:

Mystic Seaport Lighthouse, Connecticut, USA

Half-thawed ice heralds the end of winter in the historic harbour of Mystic. The 8m (26ft) squat lighthouse tower at the south end – New England's shortest – is a guiding light for incoming craft.

OPPOSITE:

West Pierhead Lighthouse, Cleveland Harbor, Ohio, USA

A harbour light was first installed here in 1831. This image shows winter ice cloaking the cast-iron lighthouse, built in 1911 to guide ships from Lake Erie into the Port of Cleveland and the Cuyahoga River. It is now out of commission.

Peggy's Point Lighthouse, Nova Scotia, Canada

Facing west on Nova Scotia's southwest coast, this scenically located lighthouse is a popular tourist attraction. The octagonal 15.2m (50ft) tower once had its own post office. Since 2009, the lighthouse has shown a fixed red light.

LEFT:

**Port Washington
Breakwater Light,
Lake Michigan,
Wisconsin, USA**

The Great Lakes of North
America are ringed with
lighthouses. This 23.7m
(78ft) metal art-deco
structure, on its arched
base, was put up in
1934–35, but is no longer
functional, and its lantern
room has been removed.

OPPOSITE:

**Outer Lighthouse,
St Joseph North
Pier, Lake Michigan,
Michigan, USA**

Thick fronds of ice cling
to the 10.7m (35ft) iron
tower and its raised access
walkway, at the end of
the harbour breakwater.
Since 2008, the outer and
inner lights have been
managed by the city as
a historic site.

Octagon Lighthouse, Eldred Rock, Haines, Alaska, USA

Built in 1906, this lighthouse's eight-sided wooden tower rises from a concrete building to a height of 17m (56ft). Since 1973, it has been an unstaffed automated beacon. A local preservation society maintains it. To purists, this is technically a lightstation; the term 'lighthouse' is reserved for free-standing towers.

LEFT:

Cape Neddick Lighthouse, Maine, USA

This tower, of brick and cast-iron construction, has been active since 1879. It is 12.5m (41ft) high; its focal height (level of the light beam) is 14.6m (48ft). The present lens was installed in 1928. Automated since 1987, it flashes red every six seconds.

BELOW:

Battery Point Lighthouse, Crescent City, California, USA

Now a museum site, the 14m (46ft) brick tower rises from a building that held oil stores, crew quarters and fog signal equipment. Operating since 1856, and automated in 1953, it has survived many storms, including the tsunami of 1964.

ABOVE:
Alcatraz Island Lighthouse, San Francisco Bay, USA
A lighthouse has been sited here since 1854. When
Alcatraz Prison was extended in 1909, a new cement-
lined tower was built, incorporating the lighting system
from its predecessor. Now fitted with a VRB-25 (Vega
Rotating Beacon), it flashes white every five seconds.

OPPOSITE:
**Castle Hill Lighthouse, Narragansett Bay, Newport,
Rhode Island, USA**
Built into the cliff face, this lighthouse is a compact
white structure, 10m (34ft) high, and emitting a red flash
every 30 seconds. First lit in 1890, it is well known as the
start and finishing point for yacht races.

OPPOSITE:
Split Rock State Park Historical Lighthouse, Minnesota, USA
Southwest of Silver Bay on Lake Superior, this two-stage brick octagonal tower has a focal height of 40m (130ft). It was decommissioned in 1969, but has since been restored as a feature of Split Rock State Park.

ABOVE:
Fort, or Admiral's, Point Lighthouse, Bonavista Peninsula, Newfoundland, Canada
A lighthouse has been here since 1874, but the present tower, although built in traditional style, dates only from 2003. Standing 22.8m (75ft) above the sea, its signal is a white flash every five seconds.

North Head Lighthouse, Cape Disappointment, Washington State, USA

Now situated in a state park, the pepperpot-shaped lighthouse, 20m (65ft) in height, went into operation in 1898 and was automated from 1961. It emits two white flashes with a 7.5-second interval, every 30 seconds.

Mukilteo Lighthouse, Snohomish County, Washington State, USA

In 1823, the French physicist Augustin-Jean Fresnel introduced a system of prismatic lenses that greatly intensified a light beam. In six different sizes, the Fresnel lens became standard equipment in lighthouses across the world. Mukilteo Lighthouse sends out a white flash every five seconds.

Point Reyes Lighthouse, California, USA
The lantern room has two walkways: one for
observation, the other for cleaning the outside glass,
which would be left salt-smeared after storms. The
lighthouse, at the entrance to San Francisco Bay, has
functioned since 1870.

OPPOSITE LEFT:
Kilauea Lighthouse, Kauai Island, Hawaii, USA
In this picture and the image of Point Reyes Lighthouse
shown left, the vent ball (used to draw out fumes and
heat from the lantern room, and to create a current of
air for the kerosene-fired flame) and lightning conductor
of the typical 19th-century lighthouse can be seen.
Kilauea Lighthouse was restored in 2013, 100 years after
it was built.

RIGHT:
**Gay Head Lighthouse, Aquinnah, Martha's Vineyard,
Massachusetts, USA**
Below the lantern room was the service room, where the
revolving mechanism was operated, with a door to an
external walkway. Gay Head Lighthouse was moved 39m
(129ft) inland in 2015 because of coastal erosion.

CORK
CITY
LIBRARIES

**Harbour Town Lighthouse, Hilton Head,
South Carolina, USA**

Completed in 1970, this private lighthouse adds
distinction to a popular resort harbour. Hexagonal,
metal-clad over a wooden framework, and red-and-white
banded, it is 27m (90ft) high and flashes white every
25 seconds.

**Montauk Point Lighthouse, Long Island,
New York, USA**

A lighthouse was first installed at the easternmost point
of Long Island in 1796. The present octagonal sandstone
tower dates from a 4m (14ft) heightening in 1860, and
was restored in 1998–99. Its daymark is a brown band,
and the light is a white flash every five seconds.

LEFT:

**Tybee Island
Lightstation,
Georgia, USA**
This is one of America's
oldest light stations,
operational since 1736.
The black brick tower,
with its broad white band,
was rebuilt and heightened
in 1866, and restored in
1998–99. Standing 47m
(154ft) high, it has 178
steps. Its white beam is
visible from 29km (18
miles) away.

RIGHT:

**North Pier Lighthouse,
Duluth, Minnesota, USA**
Standing at the entrance
to the Duluth Ship Canal
since 1910, this is a round
tower of steel plate, 11m
(36ft) tall, painted white,
with a black lantern room.
It still has its original fifth-
order Fresnel lens, with a
30-km (18-mile) range.

ABOVE:
Cape Meares Lighthouse, Tillamook Bay, Oregon, USA
Grand atmospheric effects are often seen from lighthouses. When this 1890 tower was replaced by a new one in 1963, local interests took over and still maintain it. It is octagonal, brick with iron cladding, and 12m (38ft) high.

OPPOSITE:
Point Sur Lighthouse, Monterey County, California, USA
Lit since 1889, the square tower rises from a red sandstone building that incorporated the fog signal mechanism. The light is a Directional Code Beacon, DCB-224, developed as an aero-beacon but widely used in lighthouses, emitting a white flash every 15 seconds.

Biloxi Lighthouse, Mississippi, USA
Unusually positioned between the lanes of US Highway 90, Biloxi's handsome white lighthouse was one of the first to be built of cast iron, over a brick frame, in 1848. It retains its original Fresnel lens. Now owned by the city, it underwent restoration in 2009.

RIGHT:
Rockwall Harbor, Dallas, Texas, USA
Overlooking the artificial Lake Ray Hubbard at Rockwall, this white-painted octagonal lighthouse, designed in traditional style, was opened in 1968. 10.7m (35ft) high, and with a diameter of 2.4m (8ft), it shows a revolving white light.

Portland Head Lighthouse, South Portland, Maine, USA
Many early lighthouses were shaped as the frustum (lower section beneath the point) of a cone, like this fine example. Dating from 1791, and built of rubblestone, it was raised by 6.1m (20ft) between 1866 and 1883. Its present height is 24.4m (80ft), and it flashes white every 45 seconds.

LEFT:

Lighthouse Walton, Santa Cruz, California, USA

This breakwater light at the north end of Monterey Bay was built in 2001–02. Traditional in outline, it is formed of 'shotcrete', with the more compact lantern room that modern technology allows. With a focal height of 11m (36ft), it shows a green light every 36 seconds.

RIGHT:

Hunting Island Lighthouse, South Carolina, USA

Non-operational since 1933, this lighthouse has a lofty tower 41m (136ft) high, made of bricks clad in cast-iron sections, and with a cast-iron spiral stair inside. Renovated in 2003–05, it forms a feature in a state park.

Lorain Lighthouse, Lake Erie, Lorain, Ohio, USA
Set at the north end of the West Harbor Breakwater, this square three-storey tower replaced an earlier structure in 1917. Decommissioned in 1966, it narrowly escaped demolition, and a long-term restoration programme was completed in time for the lighthouse's centennial in 2017.

Lachine Lighthouse, Quebec, Canada
One of two 'range lights' on the Lachine Canal, this was a wooden tower from 1849, and a steel-clad conical frustum from 1889 to 1900, when it got its present form. Painted white, with a thin red band, its focal height is 9m (30ft) and it displays a fixed green light.

New London Ledge Light, Groton, Connecticut, USA
A cylindrical granite and brick tower, 17.7m (58ft) high, and mounted on a three-storey base building, this was first lit in 1909 and automated in 1987. Its light is powered by solar energy, beaming three white flashes followed by one red, at intervals of five, 10 and 20 seconds.

Toledo Harbour Light, Maumee River, Lake Erie, Ohio, USA

Steel-framed and built of buff-coloured brick, this four-stage tower, 26m (85ft) high, was completed in 1904 and automated in 1966. The original light was replaced by a modern lens in 1985. A mannequin female keeper, 'Sarah', is set in a window to discourage vandals.

RIGHT:

White Shoal Lighthouse, Lake Michigan, Michigan, USA

The spiral red band is a unique daymark on this 1910 tower, 37m (121ft) tall, built of steel and brick, with a gunnite-coated exterior. The lantern room is of aluminium, with an acrylic lens of 1.2 million candela flashing white every five seconds.

Milwaukee Pierhead Lighthouse, Wisconsin, USA
This harbour entrance light dates from 1872. It has a
circular steel tower 12m (41ft) high, with a decagonal
lantern room. Automated since 1939, it flashes red
every four seconds, and works in conjunction with the
Breakwater Light.

OPPOSITE FAR LEFT:

La Martre Lighthouse, Quebec, Canada

Known as 'the red lighthouse', this has an octagonal wooden tower set on a steep slope. It maintains the original light and revolving apparatus, with the lens set on a bath of mercury, and a winding pulley to power the rotating table. It has a vertical red stripe as a daymark.

OPPOSITE LEFT:

Cape Spear Lighthouse, St John's, Newfoundland, Canada

North America's most easterly point has been marked by a lighthouse since 1836. The original wooden tower still stands, but in 1955 the light was transferred to a concrete tower in traditional tapering octagonal form, 13.7m (45ft) high and emitting three white flashes every 15 seconds.

RIGHT:

Rawley, or Twin River Point Lighthouse, Two Rivers, Wisconsin, USA

The first lighthouse here, overlooking Lake Michigan, was built in 1874. It was replaced by the pylon-style tower in 1895. Standing 34.4m (113ft) high, it was converted in 1952 from Fresnel lens to aero-beacon, with two DCB-36 lights.

OPPOSITE:

Cape Forchu Lighthouse, Yarmouth, Nova Scotia, Canada

A lighthouse has been here since 1840, but this concrete tower dates from 1962. The first Canadian light to be transferred from government to municipal ownership, in 2000, its 1 million candela beam reaches 56km (35 miles).

RIGHT:

Brockton Point Lighthouse, Stanley Park, Vancouver, British Columbia, Canada

Set on an arched base above the coastal path, this square masonry lighthouse, white with a red band, dates from 1914. It was deactivated in 2008.

Cape May Lighthouse, New Jersey, USA
Nearly three million visitors have ascended the 199 steps of this spiral since the tower was opened to the public in 1988. The brick-built lighthouse, 48m (157ft) high, is still operational, showing a white flash every 15 seconds.

OPPOSITE:
Ponce de Leon Inlet Light, Florida, USA
This image shows the metal steps of Florida's tallest lighthouse. Situated south of Daytona Beach, it is claimed to be the USA's second-highest masonry lighthouse, at 53m (175ft) high. There are 203 steps to the lantern room. Its 1904 lens and mechanism are still in use, emitting six flashes every 30 seconds.

Lighthouse Walkway, Portsmouth Harbour Lighthouse, Portsmouth, New Hampshire, USA
The wooden walkway crosses above the rocks to the lighthouse door. The light, automated in 1960, is a fixed green, with a fourth-order Fresnel lens, giving visibility over 22km (14 miles).

LEFT:

Tarrytown Lighthouse, Hudson River, New York City, USA

This landmark on the Hudson River was installed in 1883. It has a sectional cast-iron structure 18m (60ft) high, set on a concrete base. Automated in 1957, it was deactivated in 1961, but under local auspices was relit in 2015 with a replica Fresnel lens.

BELOW:

Point Bonita Lighthouse, San Francisco Bay, California, USA

The remote situation of this lighthouse is reached via a path, a tunnel and a suspension bridge. In its present form, the lighthouse dates from 1877. It is a brick hexagon painted white, and 10m (33ft) high, but its elevated situation gives a focal height of 38m (124ft).

Annisquam Harbour Lightstation, Gloucester, Massachusetts, USA

The station was first established in 1801 at Wigwam Point, near Gloucester. The present tower was completed in 1897, automated in 1974 and renovated in 2008. Standing 13.7m (45ft) high, its VRB-25 optic flashes white with one red sector.

LEFT:

Souris Lighthouse, Prince Edward Island, Canada

This square-based, tapering wooden tower is a typical Prince Edward Island lighthouse. Built in 1880, it was restored in 2009–10. With a focal height of 27m (89ft), it emits a two-second white beam every two seconds.

OPPOSITE:

Edgartown Lighthouse, Martha's Vineyard, Massachusetts, USA

Originally built on an artificial platform, sea action has created a beach to link it to the mainland. The first tower was wrecked in a storm; the present cast-iron tower (c. 1881) was relocated here in 1939. The focal height is 14m (45ft); its light is a red flash every six seconds.

East Pierhead Light, Michigan City, Indiana, USA

Local enthusiasm preserved and restored this historic light and its cast-iron walkway after it was declared redundant in 1960. The first light here was erected in 1858; the present structure, with base stores and machinery, dates from 1904.

61

Crisp Point Lighthouse, Lake Superior, Michigan, USA
Completed in 1904, and 17.7m (58ft) high, this lighthouse was officially decommissioned in 1992. Now owned by Luce County, it was restored between 1997 and 2011. Since 2012, it has operated as a Private Aid to Navigation, flashing white every six seconds.

LEFT:
Dry Tortugas Lighthouse, Loggerhead Key, Florida, USA
This is the remotest lighthouse of the United States, established in 1858. Built of brick in standard frustum form, it is 48m (157ft) tall. The light was electrified in 1933, and automated in 1988. Since 2015 it has been operated by a VRB-25 beacon.

RIGHT:
Cockspur Island Lighthouse, Georgia, USA
Originally (in 1839) this sea-washed tower was only a daymark; a light was installed in 1848. The present 14-metre (46ft) structure was in active service from 1909 to 2007; it is still lit as a historic attraction.

Bodie Island Lighthouse, Outer Banks, North Carolina, USA

The first lighthouse here was built in 1847; this 48-m (156-ft) tower was completed in 1872, of granite and rubblestone, with white and black daymark bands. Still using the Fresnel lens of 1872, it flashes white in two 2.5 second cycles every minute.

Europe

Europe's coasts are marked with an array of lighthouses in a wide range of building styles, and often in spectacular locations. Some European lights are ancient: lighthouses of Roman origin still operate in Spain (La Coruña) and Italy (Genoa), but tower-type lighthouses were extremely rare until the late 18th century. Technical advances were first led by France, where François-Pierre Aimé Argand invented the double-draught oil burner in 1782. The Argand lamp gave a much stronger light than anything before. It was used in many countries, with improvements, right up to the 1880s, normally in combination with the Fresnel lens, first tried out in the Cordouan lighthouse in 1823.

In recent years, many countries have contributed to the modernization and automation of lighthouses, using a variety of construction materials and lighting systems. However, many European lighthouses have also been declared redundant and decommissioned in the past 20 years, converted to other purposes or turned into museums. All European countries are affiliated to the International Association of Marine Aids to Navigation and Lighthouse Authorities, founded in 1957 and based near Paris, France.

OPPOSITE:
Felgueiras Lighthouse, Porto, Portugal
Resisting the force of storm waves since it was built in 1886, this lighthouse stands at the end of the old north breakwater of the Douro River. A hexagonal granite tower 10m (33ft) high, it was decommissioned in 2009.

RIGHT:

Podersdorf Lighthouse, Lake Neusiedl, Burgenland, Austria
Built in 1998, and 11m (36ft) high, this lighthouse marks the harbour of Podersdorf on this large inland lake with a fixed white beam and an orange storm warning light. There is no commercial traffic, but the lake is used by pleasure craft.

OPPOSITE:

East Pier Light, Blankenberge, Flanders, Belgium
Remnants of old jetties surround the light, whose trestle pier gives it a focal height of 12.5m (41ft). This cylindrical cast-iron tower was built in 1913, though previous lights marked the harbour. It emits a continuous red light.

OPPOSITE:

Ahtopol Rock Lighthouse, Bulgaria

This three-stage rubblestone tower on the southern Black Sea coast is set on a square, unpainted base. The lighthouse is topped by a cast-iron pylon, with a focal height of 15m (49ft). Renovation work was carried out in 2009; the light gives six short and one long white flash every 15 seconds.

RIGHT:

Stafnesviti Lighthouse, Reykjanes Peninsula, Iceland

At the westernmost point of the Reykjanes Peninsula stands this terracotta-coloured square tower, built in 1925 of concrete, 11.5m (38ft) tall, and with an octagonal lantern room.

LEFT TOP:

Pokonji Dol Lighthouse, Croatia
Dating from 1872, this lighthouse is in the middle of
the Pokonji Dol islet. It comprises a square tower of
unpainted stone rising 4.6m (15ft) above the keeper's
house. A white flash is emitted every four seconds,
with a range of 19km (12 miles).

LEFT BOTTOM:

Veli Rat Lighthouse, Dugi Otok, Croatia
Only its shadow indicates the 36m (118ft) height of the
tower. A light was first established here in 1849, and, like
some other Adriatic lighthouses, it has a resident keeper.
Its double white flash, every 20 seconds, is visible for
41km (25 miles).

OPPOSITE:

Blitvenica Island Lighthouse, Croatia
Constructed of local stone in 1879, the octagonal tower
of this lighthouse rises from the keeper's house and
stands 21m (69ft) high. Blitvenica is southwest of the
island of Zirje. The light is two white flashes every
30 seconds.

ABOVE:
Kjeungskjaer Lighthouse, Ørland, Norway
Situated north of the Arctic Circle, the light is not needed between 21 July and 16 May each year. Built in 1880, this is Norway's only octagonal lighthouse, and is 20.6m (68ft) high. Its occulting light (whereby the light period is longer than the dark period) flashes red, white and green every six seconds.

RIGHT:
Bengtskär Lighthouse, Archipelago Sea, Finland
The tallest lighthouse in Scandinavia, standing on a rocky islet at the mouth of the Gulf of Finland, this rises 46m (151ft) above the rock. Built of local granite in 1906, it was converted to wind-power electricity in 1983, and renovated in the 1990s. It emits three white flashes every 20 seconds.

Harbour Lighthouse, Chania, Crete, Greece
The first light here was built by the Venetians in the 16th century. An Egyptian-style minaret-like tower was built in 1839. The present structure, completed in 2006, is 21m (69ft) high and combines elements of its predecessor with 'Venetian' features. It is no longer operational.

ABOVE:
Burgas East Arm Lighthouse, Bulgaria
Burgas has a modern harbour on the Black Sea; this is its
secondary lighthouse, on the inner, eastern side between
the marina and the commercial port. It shows a red
isophase light (equal periods of light and dark) every six
seconds, and stands 6m (19ft) high.

OPPOSITE:
Punta Frouxeira Lighthouse, Valdoviño, Galicia, Spain
Strikingly different to traditional designs, this square
tower, 30m (98ft) high, beams five white flashes every 15
seconds out over the Bay of Biscay. The light is visible for
41km (25 miles). Operational since 1994, it is maintained
by the Ferrol port authority.

OPPOSITE:
Kiipsaare Lighthouse, Vilsandi National Park, Saaremaa, Estonia
A 26m (85ft) high reinforced concrete tower built in 1933, this was originally perpendicular and on dry land. Coastal erosion has brought the tideline up to it and caused it to tilt. It is no longer operational.

RIGHT:
Vorontsov Lighthouse, Odessa, Crimean Peninsula, Russia
The first lighthouse here was built in 1862. This is the third to occupy the site: it is a cast-iron cylinder, 26m (85ft) tall, and was first lit in 1955. Painted white, it shows three red flashes every 12 seconds.

**Strömmingsbådan Island Lighthouse,
Kvarken Archipelago, Finland**
Impressive atmospheric effects are frequent around this
lighthouse, active since 1885. It has a stone tower 14m
(46ft) tall and emits four two-second flashes every 20
seconds, white to seaward, red towards the reefs.

**Ploumanac'h Lighthouse, Perros-Guirec,
Côtes d'Armor, France**
Built of local pink granite, this tapering castellated
tower replaced a war-destroyed predecessor in 1946.
The clifftop site gives it a focal height of 26m (85ft),
and its occulting red and white beam, which it emits
every four seconds, has a range of 22km (14 miles).

OPPOSITE:

Kermorvan Lighthouse, Le Conquet, Finistère, France

The most westerly lighthouse on the French mainland, it was built in 1849. It has been automated since 1994. Its focal height is 20.3m (66ft), and its white flash, every five seconds, is visible for a distance of 41km (25 miles).

LEFT:

Petit Minou Lighthouse, Plouzané, Brittany, France

A former semaphore tower adjoins the 1848 granite lighthouse, 22m (72ft) high, on the approaches to the naval port of Brest. Automated in 1989, its 35-km (22-mile) beam flashes white and red every six seconds.

LEFT:

Camogli Lighthouse, Liguria, Italy
Replacing a 19th-century predecessor weakened by storms, this white concrete lighthouse, 11m (36ft) tall, was put up in the 1970s. The lantern was damaged in a storm in 2011 and was replaced in 2012.

OPPOSITE:

Puerto Banùs Lighthouse, Costa del Sol, Spain
At the end of a long mole protecting the marina at the modern resort of Puerto Banùs, close to Marbella, this stone-built harbour light, designed in traditional circular form on a wider lower storey, dates from 1970 and shows a fixed light.

Pointe de Barfleur Lighthouse, Basse Normandie, France

A slender 75m (247ft) tower, claimed as the world's third-tallest lighthouse, this was built in 1835, replacing an older light. In 1893 it was electrified with its own generator. The 1903 Fresnel lens emits a double white flash every 10 seconds.

Pakri Lighthouse, Harju County, Estonia

Estonia's tallest, this lighthouse was renovated in 2001 and is now a museum as well as an active light. There are 275 steps to the lantern room. Within the spiral can be seen the framework enclosing the former chains and weights that turned the optic system.

LEFT:

La Coubre Lighthouse, Charente Maritime, France

This image shows the tiled interior and spiral staircase of the 1905 concrete-built lighthouse, which is 64m (210ft) tall. Automated since 2000, its Fresnel lens shows two white flashes every 10 seconds, and can be seen up to 43km (26 miles) away.

RIGHT AND OPPOSITE:

Cordouan Lighthouse, Gironde Estuary, France

First completed in 1611, this Renaissance-style tower is one of the world's oldest working lighthouses. Built of stone, and 68m (223ft) tall, it was raised in height in 1790, renovated in 1855 and automated in 2006. Its occulting light flashes white, red and green every 12 seconds.

BELOW:
Eckmuhl Lighthouse, Penmarc'h, France
The 60-m (197-ft) high service room is reached via 227 steps and balustrade below the lantern. The castellated granite tower dates from 1890, and the lantern sends out a white flash every five seconds.

RIGHT AND OPPOSITE:
Skagen Grey Lighthouse, Skagen, Jutland, Denmark
The first light at this maritime crossroads was established in 1560; this tower became operational in 1858. Built of brick, it stands 46m (151ft) tall and dominates the flat, sandy coastline.

OPPOSITE:

Dyna Lighthouse, Oslofjord, Norway

This rather quaint-looking wooden lighthouse, partly built on piles, was established in 1875. Its focal height is 6m (20ft) and its occulting light shines white, red and green every eight seconds. Automated in 1956, it also functions as a restaurant.

RIGHT TOP:

Skallen Lighthouse, Bohuslän, Sweden

On the western point of Marstrandsön Island, this short, cylindrical, concrete structure was set up in 1944, its position giving a focal height of 13m (43ft). Solar-powered, it shines isophase white, red and green in different directions at two-second intervals.

RIGHT BOTTOM:

Rivinletto Light, Kaasamatala Island, Finland

This small concrete lighthouse, built in 1939 at the mouth of the Kiiminkijoki River in Haukipudas, Oulu, is a sector light. It is intended to help ships navigate dangerous waters by showing different-coloured lights from different angles, or, as here, a white flash visible only within the sector 016°–248°.

Urk Lighthouse, Ijsselmeer, Netherlands
Rising from the sea-wall and looking over an inland sea, this tower of white-painted brick was built in 1845 and restored in 1972. It is 18.5m (61ft) tall. Retaining its original Fresnel lens, it flashes white every five seconds.

Rubjerg Knude Old Lighthouse, Jutland, Denmark

The inexorable building up of sand dunes and advancing coastal erosion caused the closure in 1968 of this 23m (75ft) square tower, originally opened in 1900. Completely abandoned in 2002, it is expected to collapse into the sea by 2023.

RIGHT:

Harbour Lighthouse, Rethymno, Crete, Greece
Sometimes known as the 'Turkish Lighthouse', this has stood at the harbour since 1864, replacing an older structure built during Venetian control of the port. Its lantern room can be lit, but it no longer functions as a regular harbour light.

OPPOSITE:

Alanya South Breakwater Lighthouse, Turkey
Given an intentionally picturesque appearance in this holiday resort, and with a wide viewing gallery, the lighthouse was built in around 2009. With a focal height of 20m (66ft), it emits a green flash every five seconds.

Llanes Lighthouse, Asturias, Spain

On the waterfront, this low stone tower is attached to the keeper's house. It was built in 1961 to replace a temporary light after the original (1860) tower was left unusable following a fire in 1946. With a focal height of 12m (39ft), its white light occults four times every 15 seconds.

La Jument Lighthouse, Ouessant, France

The massive top section of this 47m (154ft) octagonal tower, built of granite and opened in 1911, is often engulfed by breaking waves. Its Fresnel lens emits three red flashes every 15 seconds.

OPPOSITE RIGHT:

Amrum Island Lighthouse, North Friesland, Germany

The outside gallery and lantern room are 63m (207ft) above mean sea level. The optic is a first-order Fresnel lens from 1867, now lit by a 230/250V halogen metal vapour lamp. The light was automated in 1964, 109 years after installation.

PREVIOUS PAGES:
Garðskagi Old Lighthouse, Garður, Iceland
The Aurora Borealis is often seen above the lighthouse, a square concrete structure 12.5m (41ft) tall that was built in 1897. Its light system was transferred into a new, taller tower close by, built in 1944.

LEFT:
The Brandaris, West Terschelling, Friesland, Netherlands
The first Brandaris was built in 1323. This square tower, 52.5m (172ft) tall, looking over the Waddensee, dates from 1594. Apart from 1594–1604, it carried no light until around 1830. It now gives a white flash every five seconds.

OPPOSITE:
Warnemünde West Mole Light, Germany
Two almost identical lights have marked the exit of the Warnow River into the Baltic Sea since 1903. The green and white West Mole light was resituated on the new mole in 1998. The towers emit green and red flashes respectively, in isophase at four-second intervals.

ABOVE:
Les Pâquis Lighthouse, Geneva, Switzerland
An ornate octagonal cast-iron tower 17m (56ft) tall, completed in 1896, this is a famous Geneva landmark. It is regularly floodlit, but still functions as a lighthouse, with white and green lights beamed in separate directions.

OPPOSITE:
Lindau Lighthouse, Lake Constance, Bavaria, Germany
Germany's southernmost lighthouse is a stone tower 33m (108ft) high, with machicolation below the gallery. Inaugurated in 1856, it uniquely incorporates a clock face, on the lakeward side. It gives a white flash every three seconds.

OPPOSITE:
Cabo de Palos Lighthouse, Murcia, Spain
First lit in 1865, and replacing an old watchtower, this
lighthouse is 51m (167ft) tall and built of unpainted
masonry. The two-storey base building was originally
planned as a training centre for lighthouse keepers.

ABOVE:
Prcanj, Kotor Bay, Montenegro
This 4m (13ft) black-and-white pillar marks the anchorage
on Kotor Bay, flashing green every three seconds. Prcanj
was once an important Adriatic port; this 20th-century
light replaces a succession of older beacons.

OPPOSITE:

Tamis River East Light, River Danube, Serbia
Twin towers were established in 1909 to mark the confluence of the Tamis with the Danube. Built on sloping stone platforms to allow for spates, they stand 6m (18ft) above normal water level. They were restored in 2009, but no longer function as lights.

RIGHT:

Morskoy Channel Rear Light, Kronstadt, Russia
Several lights mark the entry to this major naval port, set in ranges. This concrete tower dates from 1914. It is a 41.5m (136ft) gently tapering octagon with black and white daymarks facing the channel. It sends out a long white flash every six seconds.

ABOVE:

**Ricasoli Lighthouse, Grand Harbour,
Valletta, Malta**

Mediterranean waves surge round the eastern
breakwater. The lighthouse, of limestone masonry,
was established in 1908. It has a focal height of 11m
(36ft) and emits a rapid-interval red flash.

OPPOSITE:

Strombolicchio Lighthouse, Aeolian Islands, Italy
Perched since 1925 on the plug of an ancient volcano,
the cylindrical white tower has a focal height of
57m (187ft) and flashes white every 15 seconds. The
neighbouring live volcano, Stromboli, is also known as
'the lighthouse of the Mediterranean'.

Noorderhoofd Lighthouse, Westkapelle, Netherlands

Set on the North Sea side of the dike, this was the first circular cast-iron lighthouse in the Netherlands, erected in 1875. Standing 20m (66ft) tall, it flashes red, white and green.

Eierland Lighthouse, Texel Island, Netherlands

This red-painted brick tower, 34.7m (114ft) tall, has stood at the northern end of Texel since 1864. Damaged in 1945, its height was reduced, but its two white flashes every 10 seconds are visible for 54km (33 miles).

Torredembarra Lighthouse, Tarragona, Catalonia, Spain
Inaugurated at the end of 1999, the octagonal white concrete tower is 38m (125ft) tall, with a notably wide, and roofed, observation gallery. The light sends five white flashes every 30 seconds.

Świnoujście Mole Light, West Pomerania, Poland
The form of a traditional windmill, complete with (non-revolving blades), was chosen for this 10m (33ft) tall light, established in 1874. The light is an occulting white flash every 10 seconds.

ABOVE:
Verdens Ende, Tjøme Island, Vestfold, Norway
Situated at 'World's End', this is a 1932 replica of
an ancient tipping or bascule light, its fire basket
suspended from an angled beam that can be lowered
to replenish the fire. The base is built from beach-
gathered stones.

OPPOSITE:
Sulina North Pier Lighthouse, Romania
Inaugurated in 1887 to assist navigation in the Danube
Delta, this was replaced by a modern tower in 1983.
Inactive for many years, the lighthouse is now in a
decrepit condition. It has a gallery at the entrance level,
and stands 14m (46ft) high.

United Kingdom and Ireland

The oldest lighthouse in the British Isles is at Dover, where the remains of a lighthouse built by the Romans in around 50 CE still stand. While brazier beacons were used in places like Dungeness, which was using coal in 1616, the beginnings of modern lighthouse construction came in 1698, with the Eddystone Reef, off Plymouth, as a site of experimentation. It had wooden towers at first, but by 1759 the tapered cylindrical stone tower, designed by John Smeaton, was established as the most reliable form.

A great period of construction began in the late 18th century, when the need for regularly working coastal lights ushered in a programme of lighthouse building. The construction of lights on tidal reefs was pioneered in Scotland by the Stevenson dynasty of engineers from 1811, beginning with the Bell Rock lighthouse. Whale oil was the first lamp fuel to be used, followed by kerosene from the 1860s, and by acetylene gas from 1896. From 1899, the electric incandescent bulb came into use, although many lights were not electrified until well into the 20th century.

OPPOSITE:

Trwyn Du Lighthouse, Anglesey, Wales

Between Anglesey and Puffin Island, this lighthouse was built in 1838 to mark the entrance to the Menai Strait. A circular stone tower 29m (95ft) high, it was automated in 1922. Its beam is a white flash every five seconds.

OPPOSITE FAR LEFT:

Tynemouth Pier Lighthouse, Northumberland, England

The first lighthouse here was built in 1854; the present tower dates from 1903. Substantial for a harbour light, and standing 26m (85ft) high, its beam is visible for 42km (26 miles). Guiding ships into the Tyne Estuary, it is operated by the Port of Tyne.

OPPOSITE LEFT:

Bell Rock Lighthouse, Angus Coast, Scotland

Built on a tidal rock, this is the world's oldest surviving sea-washed lighthouse, completed in 1811 by Robert Stevenson. The granite tower is 35m (115ft) high, tapering from 13m (42ft) to 4.5m (15ft). Staffed until 1988, it uses a Dalen gas-lit optic, flashing white every five seconds.

RIGHT:

Beachy Head Lighthouse, East Sussex, England

Placed in the sea below Beachy Head, the tower was built in 1902. Constructed of granite on a concrete base, it is painted white with a red band daymark, and is 43m (141ft) high. A single-tier LED (light-emitting diode) light emits two white flashes every 20 seconds.

Perch Rock Lighthouse, New Brighton, Cheshire, England
Replacing a 'perch' or tripod beacon in 1830, this 28.5m (93ft) stone tower was lit until 1973, when it was declared redundant. It was restored as a monument in 2001 and now carries a decorative LED light in the lantern room.

LEFT:

Godrevy Lighthouse, St Ives Bay, Cornwall, England

First lit in 1859, this white-painted octagonal stone tower, 26m (85ft) high, was automated in 1934 with a fixed Fresnel lens and an acetylene burner. It was converted to solar power in 1995. The light was transferred to an adjacent steel structure in 2012.

127

RIGHT:

Rattray Head Lighthouse, Aberdeenshire, Scotland

Built in 1865 on an offshore tidal rock, this light, reaching a height of 36.5m (120ft), is supported on a broad granite base that holds the engine room, with a white-painted conical upper section. Electrified in 1977, the light was automated in 1982.

BELOW:

Whiteford Lighthouse, Gower Peninsula, Wales

This cast-iron lighthouse, 13.5m (44ft) high and set on wooden piles, has an unusual design for a British wave-swept tower. It was built in 1865 to replace an 1854 light. No longer lit, it now serves only as a daymarker.

Needles Lighthouse, Isle of Wight, England

At the seaward end of a jagged line of chalk rocks, this is a granite tower 33.25m (109ft) high. Since 1977, it has been topped by a helicopter landing platform to allow for servicing visits. Its fixed lens has white, green and red lights, flashing in sequence every 20 seconds.

St Mary's Island Lighthouse, Whitley Bay, England

Medieval monks once maintained a light here. Cut off from the mainland as the tide rises over its causeway, this 48m (151ft) white-painted brick tower, built in 1898, beams out two white flashes every 20 seconds.

Lower Lighthouse, Skellig Michael, Kerry Coast, Ireland

Once the abode of hermits, the rock of the Great Skellig carried upper and lower lighthouses from 1826 to 1870. Only the lower still functions. Its present tower dates from 1967, using a 1909 lens from its predecessor, although it is now electrically lit.

OPPOSITE:

**Rue Point Lighthouse,
Rathlin Island,
Northern Ireland**
This 11m (36ft) tower,
built on the island's
southern tip in 1921,
replaced a temporary 1915
structure. The light was
changed from acetylene
to automatically worked
electric in 1965. A new
optic was installed in 2004,
beaming two white flashes
every five seconds.

RIGHT:

**Southerness Lighthouse,
Dumfries & Galloway,
Scotland**
Scotland's second-
oldest lighthouse, this
17m (56ft) square white
tower was built in 1749
as a daymark. It was
later heightened, and
first carried a light from
around 1800. It has been
out of use since 1936.

LEFT:
**Ardnamurchan
Point Lighthouse,
Highland, Scotland**
The British mainland's
most westerly point has
been home to a lighthouse
since 1849. This granite
tower, designed by Alan
Stevenson in an exotic
'Egyptian' style, is 36m
(118ft) high and flashes
two white lights every
20 seconds.

BELOW:
**Sheep's Head
Lighthouse, County
Cork, Ireland**
A relatively recent
lighthouse, opened in
1968, this is a round white
tower 7m (23ft) high,
mounted on a square base
building, with a focal
height 83m (272ft) above
sea level. It emits a white
and red light, with three
flashes every 15 seconds.

LEFT:

Mizen Head Lighthouse, County Cork, Ireland
Set at Ireland's extreme southwestern point, this low clifftop light was installed in 1910, 55m (180ft) above the sea. It is reached by a concrete bridge. Its occulting white light, flashing every four seconds, is visible for 26km (16 miles).

OPPOSITE:

Fanad Lighthouse, County Donegal, Ireland
A lighthouse was first erected here in 1817 to mark the entrance to the Lough Swilly inlet. The present tower and buildings date from 1886, although there have been later modifications, including a helicopter pad. The light flashes white for five seconds and red for 20.

OPPOSITE:
Eilean Glas Lighthouse, Isle of Scalpay, Scotland
There has been a lighthouse here since 1789. The present tower, designed by Robert Stevenson, dates from 1824. Two broad red bands on white make its daymark. The light was automated in 1978, and now uses catoptric (mirrored) sealed beam lamps, with three white flashes every 20 seconds.

ABOVE:
Burry Port Lighthouse, Carmarthenshire, Wales
Seen here in extreme storm conditions, this harbour light, 6m (20ft) high, was built in 1842 for coal ships. With the decline in coal exports, the harbour fell into disuse, but has since been adapted as a yacht marina. The lighthouse was restored and relit in 1996 to serve the marina.

LEFT:

Bressay Lighthouse, Shetland Islands, Scotland

This cylindrical masonry tower, built in 1858, is 16m (52ft) high. Automated in 1989, its light has been maintained by the Lerwick Port Authority since 2012. Its beam is visible for 19km (12 miles).

RIGHT:

Hartland Point Lighthouse, Devon, England

Looking out to Lundy Island, this lighthouse, a brick tower 18m (59ft) high, first operated in 1874 and was automated 100 years later. With its long-range beam no longer required, the lighthouse was decommissioned in 2012 and a shorter-range LED beacon installed.

LEFT:

Buchan Ness Lighthouse, Aberdeenshire, Scotland
This light was established in 1827. Its red daymark bands were added in 1907. The light was electrified in 1978 and automated 10 years later. The granite tower stands 35m (115ft) high and its beam flashes white every five seconds.

OPPOSITE:

Belle Tout Lighthouse, Beachy Head, East Sussex, England
Mounted on the chalk cliffs of Beachy Head, this light operated from 1834 to 1902, and remains as a landmark. In 1999, the cylindrical stone tower, 14m (46ft) high, was moved back 17m (56ft) from the eroding cliff edge.

Lundy North Lighthouse, Lundy Island, Bristol Channel, England

Lundy's original central lighthouse, built in 1866, was replaced in 1897 by two lights, at the north and south ends. The North Lighthouse, 17m (56ft) high, remains, but the light – solar-powered with a white flash every 15 seconds – is now mounted on the building alongside.

Pendeen Lighthouse, Cornwall, England

Its clifftop position gives this short tower, made of concrete and rubblestone, a focal height of 59m (194ft). It was first lit in 1900. Its oil lamp was replaced by electricity in 1926, and it was automated in 1995. Its rotating first-order dioptric (refraction) lens beams four white flashes every 15 seconds.

LEFT:

Inisheer Island Lighthouse, Aran Islands, Galway, Ireland
Established in 1857, this 34m (111ft) high limestone tower has a black band daymark. It has had an LED light since 2014, with a range of 29km (18 miles) white and 26km (16 miles) red, emitting at 20-second intervals.

OPPOSITE:

Happisburgh Lighthouse, Norfolk, England
This light has been warning shipping about coastal sandbanks since 1790. Officially declared redundant in 1988, it has operated under local management since 1990. The double red-banded tower is 26m (85ft) high, with a triple white flash every 30 seconds.

OPPOSITE:

Trevose Head Lighthouse, Cornwall, England

This white masonry tower, 27m (89ft) tall and with a focal height of 62m (203ft), was completed in 1847. Fitted with a first-order catadioptric (combined mirrors and lens) system, it flashes white every 7.5 seconds and is visible up to 39km (24 miles) away.

RIGHT TOP:

Black Head Lighthouse, County Clare, Ireland

Concrete-built and set four-square on the limestone bedrock, this light was erected in 1936. Originally lit by acetylene, then propane gas, it has been solar-powered since 2002, flashing white and red every five seconds.

RIGHT BOTTOM:

Donaghadee Lighthouse, County Down, Northern Ireland

This tapering white lighthouse, built of limestone and 16m (52ft) high, has stood at the end of the harbour breakwater since 1836. In 1934, it was the first lighthouse in Ireland to be converted to electricity. The light is isophase, flashing white and red every four seconds.

ABOVE:
Howth Lighthouse, Howth, County Dublin, Ireland
The harbour lighthouse was opened in 1818 and used
Argand oil lamps until electrification in 1955. It was
decommissioned in 1982, when a new East Pier tower
was constructed, but remains both as a historic structure
and as a daymark.

OPPOSITE:
**Cromwell Point Lighthouse, Valentia Island,
County Kerry, Ireland**
This lighthouse was completed in 1841, to a design of
George Halpin. White-painted, the 15m (49ft) masonry
tower was converted to automatic operation in 1947.
The light flashes white and red every two seconds.

OPPOSITE:
Poolbeg Lighthouse, Dublin, Ireland
A long-established light on the Great South Wall in Dublin Bay, this was first constructed in 1767. Its red paint indicates 'port side' for ships entering Dublin Harbour; the companion light on the North Wall is green.

LEFT:
Berwick on Tweed Lighthouse, Northumberland, England
At the end of the breakwater, this unusually shaped lighthouse was built in 1826. It features a circular stone tower 13m (44ft) high, with a light window rather than the lantern room that later became standard. The conical roof is a single piece of stone.

OPPOSITE:

South Stack Lighthouse, Anglesey, Wales

Built on a rock islet linked to Anglesey by a 30m (98ft) footbridge, this white-painted 28m (92ft) tower was completed in 1809. First electrified in 1938, the light was fully automated in 1984. It has a first-order catadioptric rotating optic, flashing white every 10 seconds.

RIGHT:

Seaham Harbour Lighthouse, County Durham, England

Waves break over the 10m (33ft) lighthouse on Seaham's north breakwater. Completed in 1905, with black and white daymark bands, it flashes a green light every 30 seconds. A walkway around the lantern room was removed in the 1960s.

157

Porthcawl Harbour Lighthouse, South Wales
Resisting the strength of the waves since 1860, Porthcawl's 10m (33ft) cast-iron lighthouse was renovated in 2013. This was the last lighthouse in the UK to be lit by coal gas, switching to natural gas in 1974 and then electrified from 1997.

Arranmore Lighthouse, County Donegal, Ireland

A light was first established here in 1798, shut down in 1832, and relit in a new 23m (75ft) tower in 1864. This tower remains in use today, having been automated in 1976. It gives two white flashes every 20 seconds.

NEAR BOTTOM RIGHT:

Old Head of Kinsale Lighthouse, County Cork, Ireland

The lantern room, with its ventilation roof and finial, has topped the 30m (98ft) clifftop tower since 1853. Automated since 1987, it emits two white flashes every 10 seconds.

FAR RIGHT:

Flamborough Head Lighthouse, East Yorkshire, England

First lit in 1806, this 26.5m (87ft) high tapering tower is made of white-painted brick and has double walkways around the service and lantern rooms. Inside is a first-order catadioptric rotating lens beaming four white flashes every 15 seconds.

OPPOSITE:

Loop Head Lighthouse, County Clare, Ireland

The lantern room gallery, 84m (275ft) above the sea, gives airy views out over the Atlantic. The tower, the second on the site, dates from 1854 and is 23m (75ft) high. Automated in 1991, the light gives four white flashes every 20 seconds, with a visibility range of 42km (26 miles).

Although the lighthouse stands in the middle of a seaside town, to go inside is to pass into a secret world. This interior view (*pictured opposite*) of the tower looks up to the service room floor. The 31m (102ft) tower has a spiral staircase with short level sections at the window levels.

RIGHT:

Roker Pier Lighthouse, Sunderland, Tyne & Wear, England

A rugged granite tower 23m (75ft) high, its daymark bands of grey and red are the natural stone colours. Opened in 1903, and now operated by the Port of Sunderland, it has been undergoing renovation since 2015. The light shows a white flash every five seconds.

OPPOSITE AND ABOVE:

Southwold Lighthouse, Suffolk, England

The lighthouse was built in 1890, of brick with a smooth white external finish. Electrified since 1938, it has a PRL400TH lens, with an intensity of 17,100 candela, showing a rotating white light every 10 seconds that is visible up to 31km (20 miles).

LEFT AND OPPOSITE:

Spurn Point Lighthouse, Holderness, East Yorkshire, England

There have been several lights at the tip of this long and shifting sandspit; this black-and-white brick tower has been in place since 1895. Standing 39m (128ft) high, it was decommissioned in 1985 and remained empty until a renovation programme began in 2015.

Seen here in its 'abandoned' state, the lighthouse, restored and repainted, is now part of a National Nature Reserve and has a visitor centre. It is possible to climb to the top and admire panoramic views of the Humber Estuary.

LEFT:
Plover Scar Lighthouse, Cockerham Sands, Morecambe Bay, England
Built in 1847, this was the lower of a pair of lights leading into the Lune Estuary. A circular stone tower with an octagonal light chamber reaching a height of 8m (24ft), it flashes white every two seconds. Hit by a ship in 2016, it has since been restored.

OPPOSITE:
Leasowe Lighthouse, Wirral, Cheshire, England
Britain's first brick-built lighthouse began operation in 1763 and continued until 1908. With the lantern room removed, it now stands 33.5m (110ft) high. After decades of neglect, it has been restored and is maintained by a local heritage group.

OPPOSITE FAR RIGHT:
Chaine Tower, Larne, County Antrim, Northern Ireland
A replica of an ancient Irish round tower, this was built as a memorial in 1887, of granite blocks, 23m (75ft) high. It was adapted to serve as a lighthouse in 1899. The fixed isophase light shines through a window opening, with a white, then red, flash every five seconds.

LEFT:

Wicklow Head Lighthouse, County Wicklow, Ireland

Two lighthouses were maintained at Wicklow Head from 1781 to 1865; only the lower one, dating in its present form from 1818, still operates. It has been automated since 1994. With a focal height of 37m (121ft), it emits a triple white flash every 15 seconds that is visible for 43km (27 miles) out to sea.

OPPOSITE:

Portland Bill Lighthouse, Dorset, England

A lighthouse has stood here since at least 1716; this 41m (135ft) tower was completed in 1906. It has been automated since 1996. It has a first-order catadioptric rotating lens, with four white flashes every 20 seconds.

St John's Point Lighthouse, County Down, Northern Ireland Inaugurated in 1844, and heightened to its present 40m (131ft) in the late 1880s, this lighthouse has borne its black and yellow bands since 1954. Its annular (ring-shaped) lens dates from 1908, and emits two white flashes every 7.5 seconds. An auxiliary light is installed in a third-floor window, flashing white and red every three seconds.

LEFT:

Lower Lighthouse, Fleetwood, Lancashire, England

Looking more like a municipal monument than a lighthouse, this classical design dating from 1840 was intended to suit the new town of Fleetwood. The light has a focal height of 14m (46ft) and flashes green every two seconds, in conjunction with Fleetwood's Upper Light.

RIGHT:

Point of Ayr Lighthouse, Talacre Beach, Wales

Rising from the sandy beach, with no access at high tide, this is Wales's oldest extant lighthouse. It was built in 1776, although it has been inactive since 1883. Rescued from semi-derelict condition in the 1990s, it makes a bright landmark, 18m (59ft) high.

Dovercourt Low Lighthouse, Essex, England

Built on a prefabricated iron frame, with screwpile foundations, this 8m (26ft) structure, together with the Upper Light, was inaugurated in 1863 to guide ships into Harwich and Felixstowe harbours. Out of use since 1917, both lighthouses have been preserved as historic structures and visitor attractions.

The Rest of the World

Most of the world's remaining active lighthouses are operated automatically, with fail-safe systems in the event of a bulb or power failure, and monitored from a central location. Increasingly, solar power is used.

Lighthouses are perhaps the most strictly functional of all buildings, apart from military structures such as blockhouses. The aim is to raise a light to a sufficient height for it to be seen from a specified distance. There is a science of lighthouse design and signal lighting: pharology. Yet each lighthouse has its own distinct character, and in many cases lighthouses are also beautiful. This has something to do with their shape, particularly those with a gradually reducing concave curve from a broad base – a design pioneered by the English engineer John Smeaton. New technologies have extended the design possibilities, and the examples here, from every continent except Antarctica, show a remarkable variety of shapes and materials.

OPPOSITE:
Hornby Lighthouse, Watson's Bay, South Head, New South Wales, Australia
Established in the 1840s, this candy-striped tower, built of sandstone and 9m (30ft) tall, stands at the southern entrance to Sydney Harbour. It flashes white every five seconds.

LEFT:

Barra Beach Lighthouse, Salvador da Bahia, Brazil

A lighthouse has been here at Santo António Fort since 1698. The present black and white tower, 22m (72ft) tall, dates from 1839. Restored in 1998, its beam is two white flashes and one red flash every five seconds.

OPPOSITE:

Galle Fort Lighthouse, Sri Lanka

This cylindrical cast-iron tower at a corner of the old fort was built in 1939 to replace an older (1848) light. It stands 26.5m (87ft) tall, and its two white flashes every 15 seconds are visible up to 87km (54 miles) away.

OPPOSITE:

Nassau Harbour Lighthouse, Paradise Island, Bahamas

This 19m (63ft) tall brick tower is the oldest working lighthouse in the West Indies, having marked the harbour approach since 1817. Its white light changes to red when conditions are dangerous.

RIGHT:

Maria Pia Lighthouse, Santiago Island, Cape Verde

A masonry octagon on a concrete base, 21m (69ft) tall, this lighthouse emits two white flashes every six seconds. Constructed in 1881, it remains active today, though in need of renovation.

LEFT AND ABOVE:

Lengkuas Island Lighthouse, Belitung Island, Indonesia

Built by the Dutch colonial administration in 1882, of cast-iron plates prefabricated in the Netherlands, 16-sided and 61m (200ft) tall, this light is still maintained by resident keepers. The Fresnel lens emits a white flash every 7.5 seconds over the Karimata Strait, linking the South China and Java Seas.

OPPOSITE:

Crystal Cay Lighthouse, Nassau, Bahamas

This structure is a faux lighthouse; it resembles a lighthouse, but plays no part as a navigational aid. Now disused, it used to be a restaurant and viewpoint.

ABOVE AND ABOVE RIGHT:

Colonia del Sacramento Lighthouse, Uruguay

The light is fixed, and its lamp, electrically powered, emits a red flash every nine seconds across the broad estuary of the Rio del Plata. The lighthouse is still staffed by keepers. Built among the remains of a former convent in 1857, to a classical design, the bottom half of the brick-built tower is square in plan; the upper half is cylindrical. The total height is 27m (88ft).

OPPOSITE:

Puerto Morelos Lighthouse, Quintana Roo, Mexico

A hurricane in 1967 swept away part of the foundations of this beach tower, built in 1946, causing it to tilt. Known as the *Faro Inclinado*, it is now disused, having been replaced by a new lighthouse in 1968, but is preserved as a memorial of the storm.

West Cape Lighthouse, Innes National Park, South Australia

Built of stainless steel in 1980, with unusual convex sides, this lighthouse is 8.5m (28ft) high and was fully automated from the beginning. Powered by a solar panel, it gives two white flashes every six seconds.

Mersey Bluff Lighthouse, Devonport, Tasmania, Australia

A white-painted brick tower, 15.5m (51ft) high, with vertical red daymarks, this lighthouse was established in 1889, and has been automated and electrified since 1920. Its fixed 120V tungsten halogen light flashes white and red, four times every 20 seconds.

Ras-Bir Lighthouse, Obock, Djibouti

Standing 50m (164ft) tall, this circular ribbed concrete tower stands next to its 19th-century predecessor. Established in 1952, it overlooks the Strait of Bab-el-Mandeb, flashing white twice every five seconds.

Ogan Saki Lighthouse, Ishigaki Island, Okinawa, Japan
This tower is concrete, 17m (56ft) tall, and with a focal height of 62m (103ft). Built in 1983, it gives a single white flash every 10 seconds. This landmark is favoured by visitors for sunset views.

LEFT:

Entrance Island Lighthouse, Macquarie Harbour, Tasmania, Australia

The narrow entrance to Macquarie Harbour was known as Hell's Gates. This hexagonal wooden-sided 8m (25ft) tall lighthouse was put up in 1891. Now solar- and battery-powered, its occulting FA250 marine lantern gives four white flashes every 10 seconds.

OPPOSITE:

Cape Bruny Lighthouse, Tasmania, Australia

Australia's second-oldest surviving lighthouse, operational from 1838 to 1996, this was built by convicts out of rubblestone and stands 13m (43ft) high.

OPPOSITE:

Gatún Locks Lighthouse, Panama Canal, Panama
On the west wall of the Gatún Locks, signalling to Atlantic-bound ships approaching from Gatún Lake, this lighthouse was completed in 1914. The 27m (89ft) tower shows a green light occulting once every 4.5 seconds.

LEFT:

Slangkop Point Lighthouse, Kommetjie, Western Cape, South Africa
Built during World War I and inaugurated in 1919, the cast-iron structure of this lighthouse, 33m (108ft) tall, was prefabricated in England. Giving four white flashes every 30 seconds, it is visible up to 53km (33 miles) away.

OPPOSITE:
**Kamui Misaki Light,
Shakotan Peninsula,
Hokkaido, Japan**
A famous viewpoint,
Cape Kamui has had
a light since 1888. The
present structure, a
concrete cylinder 11m
(36ft) high, dates from
1960. It emits a white flash
every 15 seconds over the
Sea of Japan.

RIGHT:
**Cape Jervis Lighthouse,
Fleurieu Peninsula,
South Australia**
This striking design in
white concrete, 18m
(59ft) tall, was built as an
automated light in 1972,
replacing a lighthouse
from 1871. The lantern
room, set off-centre, emits
four white flashes every
20 seconds.

Oryukdo Island Lighthouse, Busan, South Korea
Crowning its rock like a small castle, this lighthouse was built in 1937. It was rebuilt in 1988 with a taller tower, 27.5m (90ft) high, overlooking the 'floating rocks' at the entrance to Busan Harbour. It flashes one white light every 10 seconds.

Les Eclaireurs Lighthouse, Beagle Channel, Argentina
This 11m (36ft) brick tower on a masonry base marks the Eclaireurs rocky islets near Ushuaia. Opened in 1920, it is automated, with an electricity supply from solar panels and batteries. It gives one white flash every 10 seconds.

OPPOSITE:

Ke Ga Lighthouse, Binh Thuan Province, Vietnam
At 41m (135ft), this is Vietnam's second-tallest lighthouse. The French-style granite octagon was completed in 1900 and renovated in 1975. Its light is four white flashes, every 20 seconds.

LEFT:

Raffles Marina Lighthouse, Singapore
Looking over Johor Strait and the Tuas Link (see background) bridge to Malaysia, this privately operated lighthouse was built as part of a marina complex in 1994. Standing 12m (39ft) high, it flashes white every 10 seconds.

199

**Castlepoint Lighthouse,
Wairarapa,
New Zealand**
Built in 1913 and
automated in 1988, this
tower is formed of seven
cast-iron sections. At
23m (75ft), it is the tallest
lighthouse on North
Island. Its lenses were
made in Paris, and its
rotating mechanism in
Edinburgh. Its rotating
beam gives a triple white
flash every 30 seconds.

**Disused coastal
lighthouse, Indonesia**
While many lighthouses,
even if no longer in active
service, are cared for by
local communities, there
are many others like this
one, on the coastline of
Java, that are no longer
required and are simply
abandoned.

Telaga Harbour Lighthouse, Langkawi Island, Malaysia

Operated under local auspices as a harbour beacon, the construction date of this lighthouse is not recorded. It is a 12-sided, ribbed stone tower with vertical white trim, around 22m (72ft) tall. It exhibits a short-range white light.

OPPOSITE:

Cape Recife Lighthouse, Port Elizabeth, South Africa

Since 1851, this octagonal brick lighthouse has stood on a rock foundation, rising 24m (79ft) above the beach. Its original Fresnel lens is still in use, although electrically lit. It shows a continuous white light intensified by long white flashes.

RIGHT:

Cu Lao Xanh Island Lighthouse, Qui Nhon, Vietnam

Also known as Poulo Gambir, this tower, 55m (180ft) tall, was established in 1904 and renovated in 1984. It now has a black daymark band and also includes double walk-around galleries. Its signal is four white flashes every 15 seconds.

LEFT:

Cape Notoro Lighthouse, Hokkaido, Japan

A sturdy clifftop octagon 21m (69ft) tall, opened in 1917, this light was automated in 1980 and has been solar-powered since 1996. It sends out a white flash every eight seconds.

OPPOSITE:

La Paloma Lighthouse, Cabo Santa Maria, Uruguay

This 20m (66ft) tall lighthouse, looking out to the South Atlantic Ocean, was opened in 1874. It was declared a national monument in 1976 and still has resident keepers. It flashes white every 60 seconds.

Vieux Fort Lighthouse, Guadeloupe

This lighthouse, at the southern tip of Guadeloupe, is built of white-painted concrete and was opened in 1995. Its height is 23m (75ft) and the light gives two white flashes, then a single white flash, at six-second intervals.

Dias Point Lighthouse, Luderitz, Namibia

A tapering round tower set on a narrow hexagonal base, this 28m (92ft) tower was built in 1915 to replace a shorter one erected in 1903, marking Robert Harbour in Luderitz Bay. It emits a white flash every 10 seconds.

Cape Leeuwin Lighthouse, Western Australia

Australia's tallest lighthouse has stood at the southwest tip of the continent since 1895. Built from limestone, it stands 39m (128ft) high. Automated in 1992, its halogen lamp flashes white every 7.5 seconds.

Gadeokdo East Breakwater (West End) Lighthouse, Yeondo, Changwon, South Korea
With a focal height of 38m (125ft), this lighthouse, built of concrete, sweeps up in a quarter-circle arc like the prow of a ship. Painted red, it stands at the west end of a detached breakwater.

RIGHT:

Iho Tewoo Harbour Lighthouses, Jeju Island, South Korea
Guarding the entrance to the port adjacent to the beach, these two giant horse-shaped lighthouses were set up in 2009 as a tribute to the native Jeju horse. Made of concrete, they stand 12m (39ft) tall and flash red and green respectively, at seven-second intervals.

LEFT:

**Ban Tha Thewawong
Lighthouse, Koh
Sichang, Chonburi
Province, Thailand**
A white tower supports
a broad square upper
section with a viewing
platform, topped by a
lantern under temple-like
roofs. The total height is
39m (128ft). Built in 2012,
it is privately maintained
and lit up at night. It also
emits a white flash every
3.3 seconds.

RIGHT:

**Jeddah Port Control
Tower, Saudi Arabia**
Completed in 1990, this
131.4m (431ft) structure
is one of the world's
tallest lighthouses and
incorporates a light and
an observation platform.
It emits three white flashes
every 20 seconds.

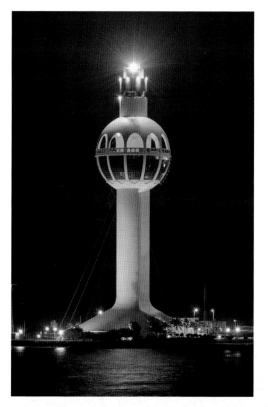

OPPOSITE:

Umhlanga Rocks Lighthouse, Kwa-Zulu Natal, South Africa

The Bluff Lighthouse was here from 1869 until 1954, when the present automatic light was erected. This 21m (69ft) circular tower carries a fixed red light to warn ships against coming too close, as well as giving three white flashes every 20 seconds.

LEFT:

Hamel Lighthouse, Yeosu, South Korea

A ribbed concrete tower at the end of a breakwater in Yeosu Harbour, this lighthouse is named for a Dutchman shipwrecked here in 1635. Erected in 2005, it is 10m (33ft) high, emitting a red flash every five seconds. Lettering in Korean Hangul script decorates the sides.

Jamestown Lighthouse, Accra, Ghana

The first lighthouse here was built in 1871; the present stone tower, 28m (92ft) tall, was put up around 1930. Its Renaissance styling gives it character. Renovated in 2011, it acquired its red daymark band as well as a solar-powered TRB-220 rotating light (four white flashes every 25 seconds). The spiral iron balustrade of the lighthouse's stone staircase is shown right.

OPPOSITE:

Vizhinjam Lighthouse, Kovalam Beach, Kerala, India

This image shows the interior of the modern lighthouse, 36m (118ft) tall and built in 1972 of concrete to traditional lighthouse design. Since a 2016 renovation, visitors can go up and down in a lift; this is the fourth Indian lighthouse to be so equipped. Its high-level light flashes white every 15 seconds.

RIGHT:

Punta Palanquete Lighthouse, Isla de Cubagua, Venezuela
Most Venezuelan lighthouses are modern; this one, also known as Punta Brasil, on an uninhabited island, dates from 2004. Replacing a concrete post light, it is made of fibreglass, 12m (39ft) tall, with orange and white daymark bands. The signal is a white flash every eight seconds.

OPPOSITE:

Cap Andranomody Lighthouse, Antsiranana, Madagascar
This 1960s-era lighthouse stands among rocky islets off Cap Miné. Repainted and renovated in 2010, it is an octagonal concrete tower 10m (33ft) tall, and emits a continuous red light.

ABOVE:

Roman Rock Lighthouse, False Bay, South Africa
This rock light off Simon's Town Harbour, inaugurated
in 1861, is 14m (46ft) tall, cast iron on a masonry base,
with a fibreglass dome. It emits a white flash every six
seconds. The attached gantry supports solar panels and
a helicopter pad.

OPPOSITE:

Abu el Kizân Lighthouse, Daedalus Reef, Red Sea, Egypt
A metal tower was first built here in 1863 after the
opening of the Suez Canal. It was replaced in 1931 by
this 30m (98ft) stone tower. Its long jetty reaches to a
landing stage. Refurbished in 1993, its Fresnel lens gives
three white flashes every 12 seconds.

LEFT:
La Chocolatera Lighthouse, Salinas, Ecuador

At Ecuador's western extremity, this 6m (20ft) solid concrete tower, pebble-coated, dates from 1960 and is a popular viewpoint over the Pacific coastline. An external ladder gives access to the light, which emits white flashes every 10 seconds.

OPPOSITE:
Cape Point Lighthouse, Cape of Good Hope, South Africa

In 1919, this square stone tower took over from the 1861 lighthouse, which was set too high up. Its focal height is 87m (285ft) and it shows two white flashes, followed by a third, every 30 seconds. A continuous red light shines at the base of the tower.

Picture Credits

Alamy: 81 (Westland61)

Dreamstime: 13 (Bryan Busovicki), 17 (Glenn Nagel), 28 bottom right (Kimberly Greenleaf), 38/39 (John Anderson), 46/47 (Rudi1976), 52 right (David Lloyd), 60/61 (Suzanne Tucker), 97 bottom (Juha M Kinnunen), 102 left (Pedro Antonio Salaverria Calahonna), 116 bottom (Melissa Schalke)

Fotolia: 213 (Igor Yu)

Shutterstock: 6 (Mike Ver Sprill), 7 (Sixpixx), 8 (Jay Yuan), 10 (Ramon Clausell), 9 (John McCormick), 12 (Ryan R Fox), 14/15 (Roxanne Bay), 16 (Ralf Broskvan), 18/19 (Sergey Uryadnikov) , 20 (Inbound Horizons), 21 (Manuela Durson), 22 (F11Photo), 23 (BST Photos), 24 (Randy Kostichka), 25 (Pi-Lens), 26 (Ivan Stanic), 27 left (Max Lindenthaler), 28 left (An Su Art), 28 top right (Nathan Danks), 29 (Melissamn), 30 (Sean Pavone), 31 (Travelview), 32 (Digidreamgrafix), 33 (Geoffrey Kuchera), 34 (Kyle Kephart), 35 (Lynn Y), 36 (Sean Pavone), 37 (Scottie Nguyen), 40 (Kropic1), 41 (Digidreamgrafix), 42 top (Manfred Schmidt), 42 bottom (Glass & Nature), 43 (Rosa Creanza), 44 (David Majestic), 45 (John Brueske), 48 left (Pinkcandy), 48 right (David Purchase Imagery), 49 (Randy Kostichka), 50 (Denise LeBlanc), 51 (Ronnie Chua), 53 (Kenneth Kiefer), 54 (Geri Lynn Smith), 55 left (Big Joe), 55 right (Ivaylo Pankov), 56/57 (P Meybruck), 58 (Arthur Villator), 59 (Melissamn), 62/63 (Doug Lemke), 64 (Dan Kosmayer), 65 (Nickolay Khoroshkov), 66/67 (Anthony Heflin), 68 (Zacarias Pereira da Mata), 70 (Radoslav Kellner), 71 (Bildagentur Zoonar), 72 (Flaviya), 73 & 74 top (Bildagentur Zoonar), 74 bottom (Paul Prescott), 75 (Teodor Ostojic), 76 (Johann Stubhan), 77 (Loneroc), 78 (Anna Grigorjeva), 79 (Oleg Voronische), 80 (Hristo Anestev), 82 (Tompi), 83 (Lighthunter W S), 84 (Ann-Britt), 85 (Ricok), 86 (Jos Pannekoek), 87 (Da Liu), 88 (Steve Sidepiece), 89 (Andres Garcia Martin), 90 (Massimo Santi), 91 (Emilia Dziuba), 92 left (Lush), 92 right (FreeProd33), 93 (Stephane Bidouze), 94 left (Aleks Kend), 94 right (Arth63), 95 (Loneroc), 96 (Bildagentur Zoonar), 97 top (BMJ), 98 (Fokke Baarssen), 99 (Thomas Skjaevland), 100 (Aphotog), 101 (Artem Gukasov), 102 right (Rallef), 103 (Haver), 104/105 (Z-Lex), 106 (Menno Schaefer), 107 (Sko1970), 108 (Henryk Sadura), 109 (PlusONE), 110 (Kamira 777), 111 (Nadtochiy), 112 (Zoltan Totka), 113 top (Smelov), 114 (Alvov), 115 (Thomas Marek), 116 top (Erik AJV), 117 (Jordi C), 118/119 (Anya Ivanova), 120 (Lillian Tveit), 121 (Catalin Eremia), 122 (Richard Bowden), 124 left (Gail Johnson), 124 right (Mark Caunt), 125 (Elaine Quirk), 126 (DMC Photogallery), 127 (Nigel Jarvis), 128 (Watkeysphoto), 129 (Nick Fox), 130/131 (Ian Woolcock), 132 (Chris Frost), 133 (Stephen Power), 134 (Spumador), 135 (Targn Pleiades), 136 (Lukassek), 137 (Simon Burt), 138 (Superschwartz), 139 (MC2000), 140 (Amy Collinson), 141 (Jax10289), 142 (Marc Andre Le Tourneux), 143 (Alexey Lobanov), 144 (Bertasius Photography), 145 (Stanislaw Zurek), 146 (Shzphoto), 147 (Simon Burt), 148 (Gabriela Insuratelu), 149 (Sebastien Coell), 150 (Magati.pl), 151 top (Jan Miko), 151 bottom (Ballygally View Images), 152 (Peter Krocka), 153 (Stephen Power), 154 (Leo Pinheiro), 155 (Helen Hotson), 156 (Gail Johnson), 157 (Steve Allan), 158/159 (Leighton Collins), 160 left (Rob Crandall), 160 centre (DLeeming69), 160 right (Capture Light), 161 (Empirephotostock), 162 (Philip Bird), 163 left (Bullwinkle), 163 right (Redeyed), 164 (Connor Devine), 165 (Phil MacD Photo), 166 (Silvergull), 167 left (J McKinlay 87), 167 right (Shaun Turner), 168 (Peter Krocka), 169 (Snowshill), 170/171 (Peter Krocka), 172 (Brian Dicks), 173 (Ian Good), 174/175 (Philip Ellard), 176 (Structuresxx), 178 (R M Nunes), 179 (David A Knight), 180 (Vicky L Heesch), 181 (Salvador Aznar), 182 (Viktor Hladchenko), 183 left (George Martinus), 183 right (Beltsazar), 184 left (Stefano Ember), 184 right (San Hoyano), 185 (Tono Balaguer), 186 (James Trezise), 187 left (Slowstep), 187 right (VUS Photography), 188/189 (K Arjana), 190 (John Carnemolla), 191 (Greg Brave), 192 (Black Mac), 193 (Quality Master), 194 (Aaron Choi), 195 (Andrea Izzotti), 196 (Black Sheep 21), 197 (David Gonzalez Rebollo), 198 (Jimmy Tran), 199 (Alexander Nikolaj), 200 (Dmitry Pichugin), 201 (Leolintang), 202/203 (Muein Mahadi), 204 (Four Oaks), 205 (D M Hai), 206 (Gontabunta), 207 (Ksenia Ragozina), 208 (Oliver Hoffmann), 209 left (2630ben), 209 right (Dirk Jan Verkuil), 210 (Igor Grochev), 211 (Aaron Choi), 212 (Nathapon Triratanachat), 214 (Jeffrey Gordon), 215 (Philip 80), 216 left (Dan Ward), 216 right (Ja is so Fly), 217 (Pikoso.kz), 218 (Pa0lo Costa), 219 (aaabbbccc), 220 (Cathy Withers-Clarke), 221 (Ju Ritt), 222 (Mark 52), 223 (I Noyan Yilmaz)